This Journal Belongs To

Made in the USA
Coppell, TX
27 October 2024

39266503R00069